THE UNDERSIDE OF THE RAINBOW

The Underside of the Rainbow © 2015 by B.E. Burkhead

Published by Raw Dog Screaming Press
Bowie, MD
All rights reserved.
First Edition

Cover: Steven Archer, www.EgoLikeness.com
Book design: Jennifer Barnes

Printed in the United States of America

ISBN: 978-1-935738-75-6

Library of Congress Control Number: 2015943029

www.RawDogScreaming.com

THE UNDERSIDE OF THE RAINBOW

poetry by B.E. Burkhead

RAW DOG SCREAMING PRESS

Contents

Chamber Pot of Gold: An Introduction 9
The Underside of the Rainbow............................11
Fly Again 13
Dream Girl 14
Dirty Poems..15
Hallways 17
Remember Myself...18
Tattoo on a Soldier's Arm 19
Play-Dough 20
Madness is Addictive 21
Passing Thought 22
5 a.m. Crisis of Being...23
Confessions of the Lumberjack Poet...................25
Before i was I...26
Discarded 27
One of a Kind 28
Wavering 29
What Would Jesus Do?......................................31
You Are Beauty..32
Chest Wound 34
Phantom Breath 36
Disturb...37
America Causes Cancer 38
Meeting at 10 a.m. All Employees Must Attend ...40
Honestly 41
Feverdream 42
For the Want of You..44
Fashioned in His Image......................................46
Flesh Tone Siding 48
Tsunami...49
Deep Inside the Malibu Dream House................50
Insomniaddict..52

Two Whores in the Night...53
Waiting...55
Beached 57
The Cost of Making It 59
Life Faded Backwards 61
All The Better..63
The Man in the Corner...65
Beautiful Way to Die...69
Influence..70
Lithium Flowers (Shot to the Head).................................71
Secret Dancers 74
For Alyssa 75
Never Last 76
The Words I Left Unsaid 77
Stumbling..78
Banana...79
Bukowski...80
MILF...81
Time Is Relative...83
On the Death of Christopher Hitchings...........................84
In-Between Moments 85
Grown Up 86
Harsh Reminders of Life 87
Gas Station Coffee...89
My Friends 90
Pockets of Perfection...92
Lullaby 94
Ghost Mushrooms...95
About the Author 97

> I live near the
> slaughterhouse
> and am ill
> with thriving.
> —Charles Bukowski

Chamber Pot of Gold: An Introduction

When I first met Blake it was during my tenure as editor-in-chief of *The Dream People*. This was back in the early 2000's, when Blake was a avid reader of our publication. He was so enthusiastic and so skilled in the arts that I did not at first realize quite how young he was at the time.

So it came to be that Blake—as a high school student—became a regular contributor to not only *The Dream People*, but also provided artwork for *Spider Pie* by Alyssa Sturgill and the *Tempting Disaster* anthology I edited. Blake also made pins for us to distribute promotionally, and designed artwork for a Dream People writing journal. We were always corresponding back then, either through email or post or just talking on the phone, and I would send him old magazines to cut up for his collage work. Then he and Alyssa started up a publication of their own, an online 'zine called *Blood Cookies*, they began publishing my work frequently, so our relationship was a two-way street.

The first time I met Blake was at the HorrorFind Convention north of Baltimore in August, 2005 just after my son was born. Blake's online persona was hardly indicative of just how bursting with energy and creativity and humor he is in person. Soon after that we fell out of touch, gradually as people do over the years, with me raising my son and growing busier with my career, and Alyssa moving away and shutting down *Blood Cookies*, and Blake moving out on his own and starting a family.

If Blake were someone to follow the typical trajectory this would be where things ended…but, no. Thanks to social media we met up again just a couple years ago. During the intervening years Blake had matured, certainly, but he had retained his vigor and originality. Even more, he had spent those years honing his skills as part of a performance poetry troupe. He and his wife and son were all at my home for dinner and an evening of conversation, and when it was over, as I walked them out to their car, Blake said something about his poem "The Underside of the Rainbow" and how he'd like to perform it for me some time.

Again, following typical trajectories in social situations with other authors and editors, I would normally abstain from such a thing. Authors always want you to read their work, always want your opinion, and so forth, but knowing Blake and having heard that awesome title, I said he should go ahead and do so right then. I did not regret it. In fact, I was blown away. Most professional authors doing readings at book signings or conventions fail to be even half as captivating as Blake was in his unprepared performance standing on my driveway in the dark.

I stared at Blake, at his wonderful wife, and back to Blake. Then I said, "So… you have any more poems?" I was sold.

It just so happens that Blake often composes his verse without writing it down, reciting the work over and over so he will be able to commit it to paper later. I'm not big on performance poetry myself, because it typically refines the performance while falling flat on the page. In the case of the manuscript Blake sent me this expectation was defied.

There aren't a lot of people who can sculpt a poetic arrangement of words from an unusual concept or unique observation. There are fewer still who can arrange these words on the page as competently as they enact them in the live arena—and vice versa. My belief is these accomplishments have been achieved because Blake works from a place of unflinching emotional honesty. Flip through as many magazines and literary journals as you want, or prowl the open mic nights, but you'll find people playing to crowds. Blake plays to the art.

Now for the the predictable bit about taking somebody under your tutelage, developing their career, et cetera: I have always been a student of those whose work I put in print. Over the years I've received multiple poetry award nominations, and it was working with people like Blake that always inspired me, pushed me forward. No matter where the art lead, no matter how unexpected or bizarre or discouraging things got, Blake's support contributed to my knowing I'd be the better for taking the journey. *The Underside of the Rainbow* reads much the same way.

Of Blake's crazed verse I can say only that, in the words of Paracelsus, "All things are poison and nothing is without poison; only the dose makes a thing not a poison." So take care with how much you read in any one sitting, and be warned that, as Blake points out, madness is addictive, never more so than in his hands.

John Lawson
Bowie, Maryland June 16, 2015

The Underside of the Rainbow

I live here, on the underside of the rainbow
where pigeon shit cakes statues in white, yellow and green,
like an impressionist painter's invisible brush stroke.
These once honored heroes, now just memories of a memory
of people who have already forgotten how to believe.

I live here, on the underside of the rainbow,
where the sidewalks are thick to death with teens
lean, mean spirited pack runners who grind their teeth and spit their minds,
living in concrete jungles of used condom leaves and broken bottle blooms,
warding their territories in brightly colored markings
warning there is danger here,
there is poison.

I live here, on the underside of the rainbow
beneath the overpass
on a yellowed and stained mattress of dubious origin,
drinking in all that surrounds me and savoring the rust,
knowing intimately the beauty of the abandoned factory
the forgotten savior of the industrial age,
now just another corpse left to rot in the gutter.

I live here, on the underside of the rainbow,
playing piano in the stripper bar,
where the track-marked girls paint on their smiles and pretend to be seductive,
while their inebriated patrons pretend they are beautiful,
each needing the others lie in a marvelous waltz,
that dances upon my hands and across the keys,

I live here, on the underside of the rainbow,
where the faded light bleeds down through the cracks in heaven,
the patches of glory burning the eyes of people
who have already forgotten how to see…

Here in this place where dreams go to die,
their delusional wreckage filling graveyards like cornfields

I LIVE HERE, on the underside of the rainbow!
and as the poet says, I "am ill with thriving."

Fly Again

We had a good time
together
riding the wind
and screaming in dark places
the places where you had hidden
all your broken parts
and missing pieces
that place
where all the misplaced marbles
go

I gathered a few of them
to keep
and can't seem to let them go
these unspooled strands of your disbelief
and unpaired mittens
full of unconquered childhood fears
lay about my apartment
like the toothbrush
you never came back for
let me know
if you ever miss them

I know
it wasn't my fault
that it all went to shit
but the pain remains
from when you put me down hard
my heart didn't break
you just snapped off its wings
and it still pumps blood fine
but I don't think
it will ever fly again.

Dream Girl

In my dream
I lay with an obese woman,
her body abundant
in the way
of the mother goddess.
I held her in my arms,
feeling her flesh
heavy against my own

she listened
as I opened up to her,
pawing at her body
like a baby,
explaining my newness,
my wanting to know

she directed me
as I ate her out,
and fucked her hard,
I used her
body to its fullest
and when I'd satisfied
my every lust
we laid back and spoke,
of carnivals
and carnal desires,
and the way of the world.

Dirty Poems

When people ask
what kind of poems
I write
I say
the dirty kind
but I know
they don't get it
my poems are dirty
the way axel grease is dirty
with the soul-staining
filth
common soap
won't touch

my poems are dirty
the way medical waste
is dirty
contaminated
with ideas too
dangerous
to be handled
without protection

my poems are dirty
like used condoms,
rain-soaked cigarette butts
and corpses in drainage ditches
disposable
but ever-present
they are what has been
flushed away
but not truly lost

a backed-up sewer
waiting
to regurgitate its secrets

I write these kind of poems
caked with dirt and decay
dirty
in the way of experienced
whores
visceral
with a bitter after taste
I bare witness
to the fall of man
and record
the notes Nero plays,
because it is a poet's first duty
to write the truth
no matter how ugly,
but it is his second
to find
the beauty
in that truth,
wherever
it may be

Hallways

They are going to tell you
about windows and doors
about being anything you put your mind to
but they won't tell you about
the hallways in-between
the hallways with doors
doors that lead to hallways of their own.
They won't tell you
about the feeling of dread
convinced you've made a mistake
somewhere along the way
unable to backtrack
frozen in that spot
looking for someplace familiar
terrified you'll never feel safe again.
But that's the trick
fuck safety
gather up your courage
and jump
right out the window which God himself opened
because you will never know
where you were always meant to be
until you get there.

Remember Myself

I am always writing poetry
even when I am not,
especially when I am not.
Those are the best poems
the choicest
private and selfish,
simple in their cruelty
indulgent, unjustified
and lost to the ether
before pen could pervert
and paper could corrupt
before edits could balance
sharpening the language
and polishing the rough edges.
They are the poems
for which I will always
remember myself
and no one will ever
read.

Tattoo on a Soldier's Arm

Hardened unformed tears
stain the white snow with blood like
naked skin and ink.

Play-Dough

when I was a boy
I tried to be normal
to fit in
like magenta play dough
into the mold
provided.
But,
there was
too much of me
and I leaked out
all around the edges
forming
strange, wonderful
misshapen seems
marking me
clearly as different
from all those
who had neatly packed themselves
inside
allowing so much
to be cut away
and fall
like amputated
bits of spirit
aching inexplicably
for the phantom limbs
of their souls.

Madness is Addictive

I miss being mad
being crazy
there was a freedom in it
a complete absolution of responsibility
and self-worth
an escape from the ordinary
wrapped in purple robes
of extraordinary brilliance
madness is addictive
and like all bad habits
its absence aches within me
I long to give in
to allow myself the weakness
to let reality drift away
overwhelmed
like dandelion seeds in a hurricane
but
mad is not the way to be
though its life is vibrant
it is a candle flame
burning out of control
it is not a way of living
but a way of dying
glorious,
wonderful,
mad
dying.

Passing Thought

It starts with the hurting
the raw, open wound
the never-clean-cut puncture
jagged and frayed around the edges
but quickly
the scabs form
even as the abscess sets in
a bubble of puss and misery
so painful
that the memory of it
can not be touched
even by the ghost fingers of passing thought.

So you retell the story
first to yourself
and then to others
spinning and re-spinning Anansi's web
until you come out on top
the victim
the innocent party
and in the telling
the pain succumbs
to bitter humor
evaporating
just another funny story
in your tell-all autobiography,
but be weary
although the pain has faded away
the wound remains

5 a.m. Crisis of Being

It's five am. and she's nothing again.
She can't believe she's real,
not if the world is as foolish as this.

Four forty and she's still awake.
One arm reaching out into the darkness,
fumbling for the one safe embrace
that will save her from her lifetime of failure.
A product of misspent time and laziness,
she has created nothing
despite all the potential in the world

Four forty-four and the words won't stop.
Her hand trembles, having already written too much.
Half-knowing, half-forgetting,
halfheartedly going through the motions,
feeling somewhat empty,
longing to be heard
in the absence of love.

Four forty-eight and she's let down all her friends.
Convinced of her own worthlessness,
sleepless and consumed by unimportance
she knows there is something more
but she inevitably forgets
until she has gouged herself too deep;
she has always been a procrastinator.

Four fifty-four and she's gone too far.
Surrounded by papers riddled with secrets
she will later drink more caffeine
and hope for something to live for,
or at least to die awake to.

"What if these are the best days of my life," she murmurs.
her spirit broken one too many times,

Four fifty-nine and she is disgusted.
The writing seems endless now, pointless
she is bone tired,
a tattered and torn ball of emotion,
on the verge of a mental breakdown.
With a negative attitude and a dark outlook
she looks to the clock, sighs...

It's five am. and she's nothing again.
She can't believe she's real,
not if the world is as foolish as this.

Confessions of the Lumberjack Poet

As I rest here in my car
outside the lumber mill where I presently work
I am
listening to a violin and piano transform
into a concerto inside my ear
as I read a book of poetry
and chew idly on an asparagus shoot.

From here I can see the faces of my co-workers,
stern, rain-weathered and sundried men
stock characters from a John Ford western,
as they move inevitably back to the mill,
and I realize
that my body is so like their bodies
tired, with the earnest tired of good hard work,

Yet, I can sense in myself a difference of soul,
for my soul aches within me with a longing
so aflame
that it is constantly in danger of devouring
every single thing it touches
leaving only
hot
white
ash.

Before i was I

Before i was I, i was invulnerable,
i was impregnable, i was indestructible
because i didn't know that I could break
i was a god until I learned to be a mortal.

Before i was I, i was fearless,
life was nothing but adventure and possibility,
i would speak out with boldness and without hesitation,
for i had not yet learned to doubt myself

Before i was I, i did not know shame,
when surrounded by a sea of laughing faces i laughed with them,
joyfully!
needing no other reason than the laughter itself to laugh.
for i had not yet learned to be serious.

Before i was I, i was kind without reason,
charitable without return, selfish but without malice.
i did not know impossibilities, can'ts, won'ts, don'ts
i tried everything!
because i was fresh, unmolded and insatiably curious.

Before i was I, i tried so hard,
to become I, to find I, to understand I,
To **BE** I,
That now that I am I,
I spend every waking moment,
trying
to get
back.

Discarded

I see you and I want you
not to have
but to hold
to taste deeply
and relish your flavor
I look at you
without age or shape
and imagine how your skin would taste
and wonder what your love cry would be
I want to fill you with pleasure so great
it breaks you
and rips all language
from your tongue
I would satisfy you
as no one has ever dared to try
and ruin you
for all which would follow in my footsteps.

I know what a terrible man
that makes me
but it does not alleviate my wanting
it is not a satiable desire
and no amount of other women
or men
could ever cure
my sad, pathetic cravings
for strange and novel flesh

So come to me,
all you discarded souls
and I will remind you
of your unquestionable beauty
if only for a little while.

One of a Kind

"You're one of a kind," she said,
as her hand traced the line of my face
I took it in mine and kissed the tips
of her fingers, each tip in its place.

I said, "You're as fair as that fairy girl
a jealous queen once saw in her glass,"
then I caught her reply in a gentle kiss
and pulled her down in the grass.

I pressed my hand to the small of her back
as our bodies entwined in the heather,
for I was one of a kind, my friend,
but she was one of the other.

Wavering

I'm wavering
I don't know what it is
that I'm feeling.
The terror
I know
and embrace
as an established friend,
the dread creeping up
from my chest
to strangle each moment of joy
with its tainted hands
before the moment can even
spread its wings

There is also
a boredom
and a frantic search
for a novel distraction
to the agitations of my head
and heart.
Disinterested
in every pursuit,
I am avoiding writing,
I know
because when my pen
at last kisses the page
these words
will slip out
exposing my cowardice
my fragility
my neurotic obsessions

It is a long way down
to the bottom of this soul
where the muck and slime
congeal into the man
who I am
and I'm wavering
all the way down.

What Would Jesus Do?

What would Jesus do?
I hear you say as if you know
In a condescending tone to show
Where you think I should go,
But low and behold
I see the man who saw
Who said, "beware of rafters,
when you're after picking straw."

See, the man I know
Brought comfort and love
Not vindictiveness and shame
He spoke of peace to those
Who'd slay the guilty in his name
He cast his lot to be among
The liars whores and thieves
But wouldn't dare sit with those
so pious Pharisees.

Now you kneel before his sacrifice
And you keep your head well hung
Then look to me with reproachful eyes,
With the clicking of your tongue
Most truly I say to you
Please ask what He would do
Because for all I see
it seems to me
you haven't got a clue

You Are Beauty

Don't you get it?
Why I want you?
Why the thought of your
naked flesh
beneath my hand
the sting of the blow echoing
through my callused
flesh
sends blood surging
through my body?
Why I pause
mid-moment
to gasp with awe
each time I pull
the clothes
from your body?
Staring at your breasts
weighty and
begging
to be
teased and twisted.
Looking at you,
and seeing
all of you
I do not glaze over
your imperfections
as you
imagine I do.
I revel in them
The sag of your
belly
the thickness
of your thighs

attached to hips
which distract me
even
as I write these words.
Your hair burning
Sonja
my warrior woman
my slave
my muse
why do you refuse
to see?
to believe?
You *are* beauty

Chest Wound

I hate these times most of all,
the small pauses before you speak,
when I fool myself into believing
we can still be friends,
that we can be more,
but if my heart could stand to look
into your eyes
it would see the disappointment
that crushes your face
every time I come around.

Your eyes are dead to me now,
pale empty portholes into the bedroom
of a captain who's abandoned ship
your polite nature forcing each response
in our usual pantomime of friendship,
as we reach the end of the story of our lives
the narration rambling aimlessly
until there is nothing left for me
to ask, but about *him*.

You will smile, illuminated and real,
till my stomach turns,
the bile rushing into my throat
and I will forget that it is my turn to speak
like I have forgotten everything else
but the roadside memorial remembers,
even as its prayers fade away unanswered
their ink weighing down the pavement
like the cigarette ash laying on my heart

I would ask myself why
why I open this wound again and again and again,

only to let you probe your digits in
and finger me like a like a drunk co-ed,
the gash in me a bleeding virgin,
but we both know this anguish is better
than our speedy lust-driven copulations
could ever be.

Phantom Breath

I wake up
dreaming about cigarettes,
the lighter
sparking in one slow
clean flick
it plays out in my mind
in slow motion
the naked flame
beckons the tobacco,
they embrace and kiss
with the intensity that consumes,
the first two fingers
on my right hand
ache and itch
shamed by my
ecstasy
I breathe in their spent passions
and
sigh…

Disturb

art should disturb
art should unsettle
not as we have come to use
these words
but in their basic sense
art should disturb
as a mudslide disturbs foundations
art should unsettle
as the wind unsettles leaves
art should cause motion
loosen teeth
art should bring action to still hearts
and tears to eyes too long dry.

America Causes Cancer

I am a ceramic soul,
cracked and broken
and these words must be spoken,
this is a token of my disrespect
for the select
so don't expect an attempt
to hide my contempt for
the new constitution
no solutions, just illusions
over polluted waters
and street side slaughters
to buy our bartered retribution
a contribution
to the holy hand-grenade church
and penguins perch
over pig sties of lies
and turn the blind eyes
to the obvious treachery
and hypocrisy
in this democracy
what an epiphany it would be
to finally see this reality bit
is full of shit
and the only answer
is America causes cancer

And what would you teach me Caesar?
crowd pleaser,
deceiver of the masses,
for in all my classes,
the subtle undercurrent passes unseen
aquamarine-dreams of the serene
pass before my uneducated eyes

lies are all they are
and by the way how far
is the star we're guiding by
and you expect me to stand by
and watch the bodies pile up,
blocking the drains
and sometimes I can't contain
all this pain
but still I remain a spirit lancer
because America causes cancer

Can this condenser of reality go silent?
Silent? Ha. I see eternity in the eyes of the violent.
if these lips were to go silent then the very stones would cry
yet I die in my ineptness
the hypocrisy of this world has made me sick
prick, smoke your cancer stick
and trick your lungs to love death
with every breath AH! Ecstasy!
father bless me
before my cigarette ash tree
and still you say
you don't know?
Skirting truth like a dancer
fuck, America causes cancer.

Meeting at 10 a.m.
All Employees Must Attend

It must be grand
for those who walk in the light
to schedule their days
and great schemes
by the path of that accursed day-ball
in absence of affection
for those of us who work
in the blessed dark
who grease the wheels of their world
long after they have been lost
to the soft confines
of their dream soaked beds.

Honestly

If you are going to write
at least tell honest lies.
You've got to be a liar
anyway
if you want to write
and not just
a little white liar,
but an outlandish,
barefaced,
compulsive liar
fluent in bollox
you can't do it any other way
you have to sell it
to believe
spinning your falsehoods
from strands of sincerity.
That is what it means
to write what you know
to pen words
that ache with truth
and resonate with experience
to make-believe
and bring everyone along
on your delusion
to lie
honestly.

Feverdream

How
can you leave me
alone
crying out for more,
begging for it?
bleeding for it
in a voice
just like my own?

Like in
that dream
I never had
of suicide
and seduction
the dream was
your's
but when I told it
I said
it was mine,
as if owning it
made me more real
as if faking a dream
gave my voice
credibility.

Because you
were my hero,
in a half-assed
kind of way
In that,
I'm too lazy
to be cool
kind of cool.

And I clung to
the coattails
of your insanity
and mimicked
your derangement.
I loved you
for hating me
enough to
love me back.

And now that
you've tightened
my noose
as far as it will go
why not push me off too?
why leave me behind
to write about
what I can't
put into words?
I thought I was really
becoming something,
but I was only high
on your slow
selfdestruction.

For the Want of You

My Scottish princess
your lips taste of heather
and honeyed-wine
as my lips
find yours
in the darkness
our tongues entwining
in intricate knotworks
bringing to life
passions
flooding the lay-lines
of our bodies
with the oldest magic
blood and fire
breath and flesh
I kiss the nape of your neck
your shoulder
the curve of your breast
my mouth questing
its peak
my tongue a darting adder
sending chills through your body
with its relentless strikes
even as my fingers
move
up your inner thigh
braving the burn
of your dragon's fire
stroking, caressing
its heat burning
their tips
I trail kisses down your bow
and across your side

tickling the curve of your hip
and returning
my tongue guiding my way
as I plunge through
your darkened thicket
to the sacred fount
at the mouth of the stream
this most holy place
where I bow low
and offer prayer
in lost and forgotten
tongues
I awaken the power
within you
with each sacrifice
your honey drips
down my jaw
I worship you
as your calls
fill my ears
my desire stands
obvious
making a mockery
of my piety
and aching
for the want
of you

Fashioned in His Image

He sat alone,
aside
from the gathering flies.
despairing, he thought
of going home,
but he knew
that path
had been closed
forever.
there was no place
for him there
cast
aside from
the only
home
he had ever
known,

he sat there
wallowing
in his abandonment,
snatching
flies
that flew too
close;
taking each one
into his
hand
and carefully
ripping
off
each wing
with

sadistic glee;
the bloody
stumps
of what had been
his own
angelic wings
twitching
with his laughter.

Flesh Tone Siding

Disconnected
drifting memories of home
sing in the jingle
of the opening before me
the feel of keys
as they drip from my palm
the metal
guiding my dreams familiar
my feet walking softly
on fear-stained wood
and broken glass
I've learned to forget
but the grain remembers
the taste of lead paint
and trapped breath
the smell of piss,
smoke and cleanser
like the memory of a believable lie
if I ever made it out of here,
I'd know
that my heart was
always waiting to admit
that I had never
actually gone anywhere
because
the gravity always leads me
drifting
disconnected
towards home.

Tsunami

Once
I wrote
with wild abandon
words
spilling out
like water
from a failing dam
words
jammed together
in savage lines
of breathless wordplay
and puns
sometimes
I miss the release
but never the work
garbage that it was
only the pure
frenetic release
of words crashing out
effortlessly
onto the page
in a mad fit.

Deep Inside the Malibu Dream House

The mother walks
on the recycled shag soul
of a people from somewhere
she can't pronounce,
cherry cough syrup
drips down from her
molded smile
onto her dress
as she cleans off
the baked on afterbirth
of Sunday night's
afterdinner
atrocity.

The father smiles,
bathing in the manufactured light
of a thousand
false sunshines
his vanilla face
a mask
of sickly sweet silicone
perfection
hiding the brutality
of the massacres
which have taken place
only moments before.

The older sister sits
completely naked
and ignored
in the lonely rhapsody
of the living room

her body becoming
a suburban legend,
the Venus of the cul-de-sac
her shapely tits
a reminder
that she is a she and
not merely
another appliance.

The baby brother rolls
in an eternity
of his own excrement,
enveloped and
encompassed by
waste
his voice screaming
like that voice
in the wilderness
for something intangible
but this urgency
goes unchecked,
unchanged
and misunderstood by all.

And all around
the toads are
exploding
and the laughing
never stops.

Insomniaddict

Insomniaddict
Fixing for another dream
Exhale, be still, rest.

Two Whores in the Night

I found her on the pier
where the midway used to be,
and the condos never came,
illuminated by the only
working street lamp for miles
she wore shorts that showed
enough of her ass to have made
Daisy Duke blush
and a coat which could not
have been keeping out
the unseasonable cold.

She looked at me with bored,
hollow eyes and asked,
"Do you want a date, sugar?"
I nodded my inclination
and watched as an almost
mystical metamorphosis took place
in her eyes
as her face became beautiful.
We walked into the shadows
her high heels echoing strangely
against the wood
her ass swaying with hypnotic motion
until the darkness took us in
to its embrace
as she took me into her's
and she kissed me.

Her lips tasted like
the mouths of a thousand other men,
I handed her a wad of bills
and she dropped onto her knees

allowing some of herself to spill out
as she took me into her.
She was not without some skill,
and in order to prolong the moment
I found myself contemplating
our silent similarities
and all the moral implications there in
until my head began to hurt
and I let go.

She coughed slightly and spit
as she rose to her feet,
"See you around sugar" she said
her face no longer beautiful,
but once more plain and hollow.
I called her by her name and
watched as her eyes went wide
first with surprise,
then recognition,
then horror.
She fled, my laughter chasing her
as she ran away down the empty pier
her high heels echoing strangely
against the wood.

Waiting

I'm waiting for you
just inside the door
to slam your body against the wall
to cover your mouth
in bruises
pressing my body against yours
trapping you there
as my tongue works its way
into your mouth

To rip your clothes apart
until the remnants hang from your arms
as I assault your breasts
pulling
twisting
savagely grinding against you
my pleasure digging into your belly

To drag you to the couch
or the bedroom,
the kitchen table, or the floor
binding your arms
in your shredded shirt
forcing you down, spread and exposed
my teeth marking you
claiming your flesh as mine
my tongue and hands finding every secret
sensitive place
to plunge my fingers deep
into your gushing sex
flaming hot and feral

To take your hair in my fist
and pull until you moan
and then
and only then
to work my way inside your pussy
ridged and aching
sliding into the deepest point
then backing out
and thrusting back again
harder and harder
slamming against you with brutal force
our voices melding
into a single solid scream
of pure animal pleasure

I'm waiting for you,
go on
open the door...

Beached

Walking slowly
across the boardwalk,
the word wood
doesn't seem complete,
to cover the ruff-hewn
and fire-licked
lines in the sand,
laid down like
the carapace
of a massive centipede
left to bleach
in the spotted sunshine.

The walkway is
over-crowded
and I get lost
surrounded by
barely-legals
barely-covered,
and I think
of Cadbury bunnies
coated in gasoline,
but don't remember
where I,
or the metaphor
was going.

Feeling like driftwood,
searching for footing
in the sand
as it slides out
from under
shifting and sinking

struggling from the desert
to the water,
and I get the feeling,
that for once
something
is really happening
all around me
that each footfall
carries meaning
that the seabirds
speak with God's own voice
and truth is bubbling
from the sand
as the surf recedes
but I am
drunk
again
on this vibrant
psychosis.

The Cost of Making It

winding down
exhausted
broken by the tarot's spread
always feeling as if
something lies undone
some forgotten chore
nagging at your mind
I am a molted feather
held aloft by caffeine
questioning the worth
of living this way
working through the night
for that extra dollar
that makes the difference
between survival and oblivion
and the empty hours
which afford me
my sacred scribblings
time to render
from my thoughts
and emotions
the work that defines me
the costs to my body
and family
are felt most acutely now
in the darkness
when my flesh begs for sleep
underlining
the constant struggle
between gainful employment
and a need for art
this is what it means to be an artist

to stack the numbers
and find the work
outweighs
the cost of making it.

Life Faded Backwards

Father says his neck hurts,
and I take a stab at comforting him
but his face shifts away, searching the dust
staring out at the dying fields
he told me stories once,
of when there were angels,
and the grass grew green,
not yellow
but,

without angels everything fades,
the light draining back towards the sky,
like the souls who
rise from hot pavement
when the rains come down,
but even clear,
everything grays

like the flowers around mother's grave
withering steadily,
fading as the hope drains out of them,
like father's skin,
the color leaking out of it in tears of pure blue,
dripping down from his sepia eyes
till there is no more light,

when the angels left the faded sky,
like the air's veins had been slashed and drained
like mother in her bathtub,
hair swaying gently in the water, too pink
a red to have been filled
with real blood

the same black
rushing from father's neck
the steel gray slashed against
his skin's own,

And when
father's face shifted again,
his eyes slowly searching for me,
his cheeks flushed scarlet,
as the life faded backwards,
and the last light went out,
one,
by one.

All The Better

I speak to you in soothing tones,
a lamb so lost and cold,
it flutters something deep inside
but I still brave the temptation,
so delicate, your flower form,
I could break you with a word,
I want to hold you safe,
from myself and for myself
and as one wins, so must one loose,
my charms work their beguiling spell
and I tell you all you want to hear,
all the better to kill you with my dear

We start to kiss and I'm lost,
the taste of you drives a lust in me
so foreign to this long silent heart
I am famished for you,
I want you like I have desired nothing else,
the flimsy restraint I have so delicately balanced
comes crashing to the floor
of your bedroom as our bodies entwine,
I nip and bite and nibble hard,
what big teeth you have, you sigh
and I pant into your ear,
all the better to kill you with my dear

I make an effort to breathe,
but nothing comes to mind
your body sighs, your eyes turn cold,
drinking too deeply, I'm being sucked into the void of you,
the empty space where your arms used to be
hold me close
as I rip the life from your neck,

B.E. Burkhead

gravestones singing in the background,
my pretensions lie abandoned,
wrapped in the ecstasy of damnation,
I have no need for any weapon,
but the body God gave me to fear,
all the better to kill you with my dear.

I slip deeply into the coma of your death,
and stumble off with dark intent,
another maiden yet to wander
into my lair of spider webs,
I can not sate, it never dies,
no rest for wicked souls like me
my many loves do not remove
the passion now so fully spent,
I will find another unknown you
I will charm and then beguile
and tell you all you want to hear,
all the better to kill you with my dear.

The Man in the Corner

There's a man,
by himself,
all alone,
in the corner,
in a suit,
at the party,
who is always,
polite.

In conversation,
a gentleman,
who is always,
a pleasure,
though he's nervous,
his stammer,
is ever,
so slight.

Now he sits,
by himself,
all alone,
in the corner,
turning ,
by shades,
so faintly,
to white.

And he twists,
and he fidgets,
and he pulls,
at his collar,
which it seems,

has grown,
increasingly,
tight.

Now the party's,
forgotten,
the lone man,
as harmless,
but all,
my dear children,
is not,
what it seems.

For the party's,
reminded,
at once,
of his presence,
as he bolts
from his chair
lips open,
to scream.

And they turn,
as if one,
and look,
to the corner,
to see him,
there standing,
flesh rent,
at the seams.

And the things,
which are teeming,
and writhing,
within him,

are nightmares,
unseen,
in all of their,
dreams.

These pale
massive maggots,
all covered
with hooks,
with too human,
faces,
their eyes mad,
with need.

And the man
in the corner
sobs
without sound
as their teeth,
bore their way
through meat
and through tweed.

The screaming,
begins,
as they pop,
from his flesh,
and they wriggle,
towards the party,
with alarming,
speed.

And the man,
at the party,
all alone,

in the corner,
mouths out,
I love you,
to his beautiful,
seed.

Beautiful Way to Die

Once I had a golden voice
and I sang so deep and proud
so I drank away my blessings
and I smoked it to a growl

Now I howl at the moon each night
serenading that silver whore
and I drink the bar mats dry
'till I'm no good even to her

And I stay awake drunk and naked
writing poems I can not read
full of love and ecstasy
and unrequited need

And I fill your head with romance
for that is all I've left to give
it's a beautiful way to die
but a terrible way to live.

B.E. Burkhead

Influence

The first song I remember loving
was the second to last
on the flip-side of a black vinyl album
called Bookends
the words dark
with their hazy shade of winter,
leaves of brown,
and a foreboding sense
of something I was too young to understand.

As the years tumbled along
my tastes stretched and changed
mutated
and changed once more.
Things I once loved
seem as strangers to me now.
But I still love those dark words
and that haunting melody
though
I still feel that foreboding
something
I don't quite understand
I really don't give a damn anymore
I just love it
honestly, selfishly
without whys or any other
stupid label
as all such raven-faired beauties
should be loved.

Lithium Flowers
(Shot to the Head)

Double helix grooves
of glittering DNA
shatter as they
strike my
bones.
Petals of
brain tissue and blood vessels
burst into blooms
in spiral patterns
inside my
eye.

Somewhere,
someone
is speaking
aborted words
stillborn
from their
disembodied mouth,
their unbidden
vocalization,
a miscarriage
of noise
and sanity
dripping
from cunt lips
like infected
semen.

Liquid shit
claws its way

from within me,
ripping at
my bowels
as it too
abandons
my dying soul.

In my nightmare
of heaven
deformed angels
scream
uncontrollably
as they snap
their superfluous
bones into place,
spreading their legs
and their wings,
to piss upon
the heads of
the damned.

My ears
drip bloody joy
in response
to their song
and the laughter
ripping
through me,
eviscerates me
as seedlets
of bone
and flesh
drip out
the birth canal
exit wound

in the side
of my head.

And now
I know
that my
composted
manic-depressive
consciousness
is the perfect
soil
in which to plant
salvations
and lithium flowers...

Secret Dancers

I saw the words
dance as if no one sees you
painted on a wooden box
but the words were wrong
everyone dances that way
secretly hoping
someone, somewhere
is watching
and will see them
and will recognize
and appreciate
how fantastic
their dancing is

But we are not like that,
you and I,
we are the secret dancers
and we dance invisible
but for our shadows
all eyes fixed
on that shapely assistant
no one turning
to see us twirl and cavort
happy
unnoticed
our illusion perfected.

For Alyssa

Black haired girl dancing 'round,
the winter farm without a sound
at her feet corpses abound
pick one up, look what she's found:
Even as the season ends,
dead squirrels make such lovely friends.

Never Last

(dedicated to M. Arnzen)

I married a hooker named Charlotte,
in a silent ceremony on the pier
we spoke no words, our eyes said it all,
through the gags, the sobs and the tears.

Then they sent us on our honeymoon
and I confess we stayed where we went
at the bottom of Baltimore harbor
with our luggage of heavy cement

Now our eyes have been eaten by fish
and the flesh gone with years past
but I have to laugh at us here together,
for they swore it never would last.

The Words I Left Unsaid

Bathed in darkness
I told her I had given my heart
to someone else
words which had never been mine to speak before
unfamiliar,
they lay heavy on my tongue
 and tore at my heart.
I held her in my arms and felt ashamed
at my own enjoyment,
of feeling her body so close to mine
and at my selfish desire
to find the words to make whole
what I had so freshly shattered.

But she needed comfort,
not prose
and all my accomplishments were made useless
more than ever she needed those three words
which I had never said,
and she had never said,
but clearly now she had always meant.
My heart tugged at me to say them
for all the lie they would be
unaccustomed as I was
having broken no hearts before this one
even knowing the lie would only
hurt her more
because I was a poet,
an alchemist of language
and I found myself
at a loss for words.

B.E. Burkhead

Stumbling

they told me
throw your burden on God
but I never mastered the knack
I was selfish with my burden
unable to let go
to trust
that God could love me
if I could not love myself
and our relationship
decayed
I spent our time together
avoiding the topic
unable to approach it
without feeling ashamed
worthless
and so I looped around
caught in a cycle
of shame and personal vilification
trapped on the other side
from God's love
quietly falling down.
Unwilling to share my millstone,
I broke under its weight
despairing in the light
I named myself monster.
I stumbled
and did not catch myself
or try to rise again
and the holy shepherds
their hearts so full of fear
hid in the shadows
and left me for dead.

Banana

When I was much younger
my father traveled to Costa Rica
with hammer and nail
to rebuild the sacred places
fallen when the ground quaked
I remember being filled with envy
and with pride as he flew away.

When he returned he carried
a hat for me, a pocket of foreign coins
and a suitcase full of undeveloped film.
But he held more precious souvenirs:
the friendship of people whose language he did not share
the sight and sound of being consumed by a rain forest
the feeling of bathing beneath a waterfall
and the taste of a freshly picked
vine-ripened banana
sweeter than honey against his tongue.

Now I have wrapped my arms around the California Redwood,
I have gazed into a fog-bound valley
like an ocean of clouds breaking against the mountains
I have friends in places I have never seen
and I have felt the warm monsoon rain against my naked skin,
yet, I have never tasted anything so sweet
as my father's memory
of that one banana.

B.E. Burkhead

Bukowski

You've got to piss on the heads
of your heroes, but
I still like Bukowski
even when he's wrong
or a misogynist asshole,
Hell,
maybe because of it
you have to say something
even if it's the wrong thing
you have to have the balls to say it,
so in spite of his hero worship
of Hemmingway
his elitist devotion
to Dostoevsky
and his romanticism of the unread genius,
I like him
I like his style
he got me through some dark times
when I didn't know
who or what I was
and although I doubt he would approve
of the man I found there
that's OK,
piss on him.

MILF

You excite me
woman
mother
from the honest sag
of your suckled breasts
to the pleasant curve
of your birthing hips

You excite me
my teeth eager to sink
into the tender flesh of your neck
drawing my tongue along its wrinkles
to draw you close
my hands full of you
grasping firmly your ample rear
caressing with hands blind to cellulite

You excite me
with your thick thighs parted
and bosom exposed
dripping with dew
and nectar so sweet
my belly starts to growl
a feral sound my throat echos
I want your dishpan hands
firmly gripping my manhood
as I kiss your scar
with a lover's lips
the place where you parted
and our boy came into this world

You excite me
in loose comfortable clothes

or tight binding knots
though every assurance
falls on ears clouded by inner lies
I know your body is far from perfect
but it doesn't matter
because you excite me
Woman,
Mother
You.

Time Is Relative

Six seems such
a small
fraction
of sixty
even smaller
of five-
hundred and forty
until,
there are six
minutes left
in the last hour
of the work
day
and then
each second
seems
an endless forever.
Would that
all my minutes
with you were
as these eternities,
instead
of as fleeting
as those six
minutes before
I must rise
each
morning.

On the Death of Christopher Hitchings

Today a mortal died
named for a savior
he chose to pick up his sword
and battle Gods imagined.
Now he rests
in the unresolved
after
this man,
this god slayer
his tongue forever still
his words
both his truth and his folly
echoing on after.
Their master
wrapped
in nothingness eternal.
Rejoice
for his reward
was received in full
and relished
with abandon.

In-Between Moments

I look at you
perched on the arm of the couch
reading Lovecraft
in clothes too comfortable to be called sexy
and I realize
that these are the moments I would miss most
if you were to leave
not the wild consuming firestorm of our sex
or the universal collides of our discussions
but these still, ordinary, in-between moments
before then, but after now,
when we are quietly together
or chatting about our day
or shopping for spaghetti.

I see in these moments
all the tiny innumerable chores of life
I have surrendered silently to you
which I would need do
for myself once more
and my so called freedom seems
too reasonable a cost
for all I have gained
a different kind of freedom
to be my true self,
without make-up or performance
knowing there is enough love for us to share
not in the dull stagnation of the comfortable
but in the thrilling afterglow of satisfied passions
these are the moments that make life worth living
and more, worth living with you.

B.E. Burkhead

Grown Up

My wife and I are ten again
we make Kool-aid
in the absence of children of our own
or the imprisonment of children
belonging to others
we make jello
and cookies
and keep candy around the house
we dress in costumes
and have toys to put in our bathtub

Other people would buy sports cars
and motorcycles
or sleep around
or buy exotic pets
but we have become ten-year-olds

Except, we have become ten-year-olds
who never have to finish our vegetables—
unless they're delicious—
who eat ice cream whenever we want too
and stay up well past our bed times
in short we are who we wanted to be
when we were ten.

Harsh Reminders of Life

I fart, and am harshly reminded
of many things
feeling somewhat emptier
somewhat colder for the experience.

Some people would say they pass gas,
or have flatulence
but I have never been of that sort
I have never felt the need to white-wash my graves
unashamed of the physicality of my body
capable of producing many unpleasant aromas, yet
I am enamored to embrace them as my own
and not cower in shame behind
the violent stench of clean
and imitation flowers.

Conversely,
I do not break wind, or let one rip
I do not cut the cheese
I do not make light of it in crude phrase or gesture
knowing it deserves no great remembrance
that it is merely a moment
which, to lure the pun,
must pass.

This is why I say, "I fart"
it is a harsh word,
a cruel word,
a halting word,
but it is an honest word
allowing for no ambiguity
neither boastful nor embarrassed
it is merely an expression

B.E. Burkhead

like any other, except in that
it reminds me
that I am not merely the mind
but also the body,
not only the soul
but also the flesh

I fart, and I am harshly reminded
that I am ALIVE
in this moment, apart from all others
and I rejoice in that realization.

Gas Station Coffee

She asks me,
"When was the coffee made?"
but I don't know
so I lie to her
and tell her
what she doesn't want to hear.
She sighs then
loudly
as if the coffee's excessive age
has dropped the weight
of it down
at last on her shoulders.
She adds three
kinds of sugar
to our crap coffee
and puts it, milky white
into the microwave
and I can only imagine it
curdling
inside the sacred paper cup.
She hands me money
and I return her change
but not really
change
nothing has changed
at all.

My Friends

For all
my bitching
and complaining,
for all my
condescension
and hypocrisy,
thank you
for your patience,
thank you
for your virtues
they have
made it possible
for me
to be the bastard
to be the witty
son of a bitch,
to be clever
when cunning
would be more prudent
to show off
and then bask
in the afterglow
and so
for every time
I got away with murder,
and every line
I shamelessly stole
my friends
I owe all that I am
to you,

thank you
in every possible
horrible
way.

Pockets of Perfection

Pollen hangs
thick and lazy in the air
like glowing motes of fire
in the early morning
haze
here in the before
luscious with silence
waiting
breathlessly
for a car to pass
or a breeze to blow
for something ordinary
to shatter the perfect still
to unravel
the spider web illusion
and drag it all
crashing into the now.
Giddy
with the dread of it
until

At last it happens
First, one car,
then two,
and the spell is broken
the new day is born
and life resumes its normal
frantic squandering.

Yet, it is enough
these small pockets of perfection
these tiny bubbles of unwavering beauty
in the flawed glass

if they were more
we would live our lives stationary
frozen in rapture
and in awe.

Lullaby

Hush, hush my baby time to let sleep win,
Your grand battles to renew another day,
Your belly is full and you are dressed for sleep,
Your toys are all safely tucked away,
Tomorrow's sun shall restore your vigor,
And you will find new games to play,
Let my voice close your sagging eyes,
Rock in my arms to my heart's sway,
As we lay in darkness where nightmares lurk,
I will keep them all at bay,
Though you can not know what my words may mean,
I will guard you while you dream.

Ghost Mushrooms

Some words are always left unspoken,
some things are always left to trust,
and seeds of truth get cast all over,
the ash to ash and dust to dust.

Maybe when all ties are broken
-blood brothers and forget-me-knots-
honesty finds us bolder
as all that was decays and rots.

So plant your hopes and confessions,
unspent passions and salvation blooms,
gather up all your unresolved carnations
and loose them over other tombs

For when this wicked heart stops beating,
my honor will not be yours to save,
just bury me in a field of wild presumptions
and plant ghost mushrooms on my grave.

*Just bury me in a field of wild presumptions
and plant ghost mushrooms on my grave...*
B. E. Burkhead

About the Author

Born dead to a barren woman, B. E. Burkhead is a poet, writer and artist. He lives on the vestigial tail of Maryland with his wife, son and an army of starving cats. The Underside of the Rainbow is his first published book of poetry.

www.ingramcontent.com/pod-product-compliance
Lightning Source LLC
Chambersburg PA
CBHW022108040426
42451CB00007B/174